D0787101

WITHDRAWN

Fact Finders®

The Story of the
Civil War

Reconstruction:
Outcomes
of the Civil War

by Susan S. Wittman

CAPSTONE PRESS
a capstone imprint

Fact Finders Books are published by Capstone Press,
1710 Roe Crest Drive, North Mankato, Minnesota 56003
www.capstonepub.com

Copyright © 2015 by Capstone Press, a Capstone imprint. All rights reserved. No part of this publication may be reproduced in whole or in part, or stored in a retrieval system, or transmitted in any form or by any means, electronic, mechanical, photocopying, recording, or otherwise, without written permission of the publisher.

Library of Congress Cataloging-in-Publication Data
Wittman, Susan S.
  Reconstruction : outcomes of the Civil War / by Susan S. Wittman.
    pages cm.—(Fact finders. The story of the Civil War)
  Includes bibliographical references and index.
  Summary: "Discusses the Reconstruction period (1865-1877) after the American Civil War, including the rebuilding of the South and the establishment of laws protecting the rights of African-Americans"—Provided by publisher.
  ISBN 978-1-4914-0724-0 (library binding)
  ISBN 978-1-4914-0728-8 (pbk.)
  ISBN 978-1-4914-0732-5 (ebook pdf)
  1. Reconstruction (U.S. history, 1865-1877)—Juvenile literature. I. Title.
  E668.K74 2015
  973.8—dc 3   2014007638

Developed and Produced by Focus Strategic Communications, Inc.
  Adrianna Edwards: project manager
  Ron Edwards, Jessica Pegis: editors
  Rob Scanlan: designer and compositor
  Karen Hunter: media researcher
  Francine Geraci: copyeditor and proofreader
  Wendy Scavuzzo: fact checker

Photo Credits
Corbis: 8; Deborah Crowle Illustrations, 5, 17; The Granger Collection, NYC, 15, 25, 26, 27; Library of Congress: Prints and Photographs Division, 7, 9, 13, 20; North Wind Picture Archives, 10, 19, 22; Shutterstock: Cristophe Boisson, cover (bkgrnd), Tribalium, cover (top, bottom)

Printed in the United States of America in Stevens Point, Wisconsin.
032014 008092WZF14

TABLE OF CONTENTS

CHAPTER 1

THE CIVIL WAR ENDS

It was the morning of April 9, 1865. A defining moment in U.S. history had just occurred. Confederate General Robert E. Lee had surrendered to Union General Ulysses S. Grant. Lee's surrender ended the U.S. Civil War that had lasted for more than four years. The Confederate Army had been overpowered. Lee knew his troops could not continue fighting. The generals met in Appomattox Court House, Virginia. For nearly two hours, General Grant wrote the terms of surrender, which both generals signed. The Civil War was over.

The Union and the Confederate States of America had been fighting since 1861. The Civil War started when 11 Southern states seceded from the Union. They wanted to govern their own country. Confederate leaders thought the federal government had too much power. They believed more power should go to the states. President Abraham Lincoln disagreed. He did not think the Constitution allowed states to leave the Union. During the war that followed, hundreds of thousands of Americans lost their lives.

secede: to withdraw formally from a group or an organization, often to form another organization

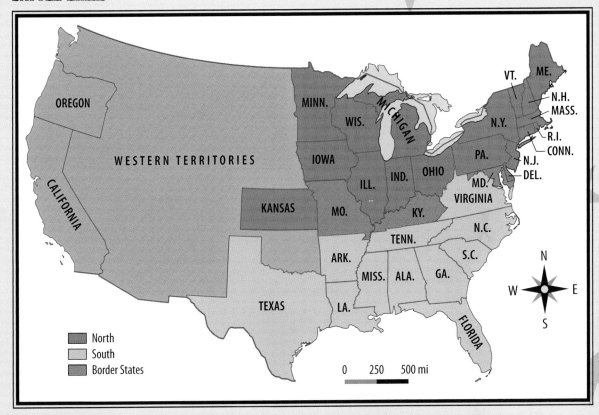

The 11 Southern states that left the United States in 1860–1861 are shown in gray. The Northern states are shown in blue. The border states (green) did not leave the Union, but they were slave states.

FAST FACTS

More Americans lost their lives in the Civil War than in any other war fought by the United States. For many years historians believed that about 620,000 soldiers died in the Civil War. But recently experts think that the number of deaths is closer to 750,000.

Picking up the Pieces

Following the Civil War, Americans worked to rebuild the nation. This time is known as the Reconstruction Era. It lasted for 12 years, from 1865 to 1877. The Southern states and their governments also had to be rebuilt. The challenge to keep the Union together did not end with the war.

Lincoln wanted to bring the Union together peacefully. However, he was faced with difficult questions. How could he reunite the North and the South? How could he ensure the rights of 4 million freed black people to attend school and get jobs? Lincoln was thinking about these problems long before the war ended.

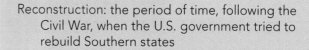
Reconstruction: the period of time, following the Civil War, when the U.S. government tried to rebuild Southern states

6

"Emancipation" means freedom. Lincoln worried about how the end of slavery would affect black men and women and their children.

LINCOLN BEGINS RECONSTRUCTION

The Ten Percent Plan

Lincoln wanted to make it easy for Southern states to return to the Union. In December 1863 Lincoln announced the "Proclamation of Amnesty and Reconstruction." He said that if 10 percent of a state's voters pledged loyalty to the Union, the state could return. It could also have a new government. Lincoln's plan was known as the "Ten Percent Plan."

Citizens of Charleston, South Carolina, are shown taking the Oath of Allegiance following the Civil War.

Some members of Congress were shocked. They disagreed with Lincoln's plan. They stated that 51 percent of white men in each state should take the loyalty oath. They believed Confederate officials had no right to vote or hold public office. These members wanted strict control of the Southern states. They were known as Radical Republicans.

The 51 percent bill passed, but Lincoln vetoed it. He did not want to slow down Reconstruction. But Lincoln did not live to see the Southern states rejoin the Union. On April 14, 1865, he was shot by John Wilkes Booth. Lincoln died the next day.

Actor John Wilkes Booth shot Lincoln at Ford's Theater in Washington, D.C.

Congress: the government body of the United States that makes laws, made up of the Senate and the House of Representatives

oath: a serious, formal promise

veto: the power or right to stop a bill from becoming law

Supporting Freed Slaves

The 13th Amendment

students at a Freedmen's Bureau school in Mississippi in the 1860s

The 13th Amendment to the Constitution abolished slavery throughout the United States. It was approved January 31, 1865. The amendment said slavery could not exist unless it was a punishment for a crime. Former Confederate states had to approve the amendment in order to rejoin the Union. The amendment was officially adopted in December 1865.

The Freedmen's Bureau helped many Southerners after the war. But its most important task was to help former slaves. Many people relied on the Bureau. It helped people find emergency shelter, food, or clothing. It also provided medical care and legal advice. The Freedmen's Bureau tried to help black people get land. It helped open schools in black communities.

abolish: to put an end to something officially

Forty Acres and a Mule

During the war thousands of black refugees had followed General William T. Sherman's army. In January 1865 Sherman and Secretary of War Edwin M. Stanton met with leaders of the black community in Savannah, Georgia. They discussed the future of former slaves.

Garrison Frazier was a former slave who had bought freedom for himself and his wife eight years earlier. He spoke for the group: "The way we can best take care of ourselves is to have land, and turn it and till it by our own labor ... We want to be placed on land until we are able to buy it and make it our own."

Four days later Sherman issued Special Field Orders, No. 15. The order called for seizing about 400,000 acres of land stretching from South Carolina to Florida. It would be turned over to newly freed black families. Each family would receive a 40-acre (16-hectare) plot. Anyone who needed a mule could borrow one from the army. The plan seemed like fitting compensation for the former slaves. But it never came true. Most black people received nothing.

CHAPTER 3

POLITICAL TUG-OF-WAR

After Lincoln was killed, Vice President Andrew Johnson became president. President Johnson had different ideas about Reconstruction. He thought the president should control Reconstruction, not Congress. The Radical Republicans thought Johnson would be tough on the Southern states. They hoped he would follow their Reconstruction plan. But they were wrong.

Johnson let former Confederate states rejoin the Union. The Radical Republicans were angry. They were shocked when he pardoned former Confederates. And they were worried when Johnson recognized the new state governments. Their hopes for changing the South were destroyed.

FAST FACTS

Andrew Johnson was the only Southern senator to remain loyal to the Union at the start of the Civil War. He was considered a traitor among Confederates.

pardon: to forgive someone officially for a serious offense

President Andrew Johnson

Defining Freedom

During Reconstruction Southern states passed laws called Black Codes. The purpose of Black Codes was to deny African-Americans equal rights. This kept them under the control of whites. Black Codes made African-Americans second-class citizens. In some states, they could work only as servants or farm hands. They could not own guns, serve on juries, vote, or travel freely. Black Codes challenged what freedom really meant for freed slaves.

Battle at the Capitol

The Radical Republicans held their ground. They had no use for a president who did not believe in racial equality. They passed bills that protected the freedoms of former slaves. One of the bills was the Civil Rights Act of 1866. This bill declared that all people born in the United States were citizens and had equal rights. Congress also passed a second Freedmen's Bureau Act. It kept the Freedmen's Bureau going for two more years. It also put the federal government in charge of protecting African-Americans.

Johnson showed his power. He vetoed the bills. He thought the bills went against the Constitution and took away the rights of whites. Congress challenged his vetoes. The laws were passed with a two-thirds vote. This was the first time in U.S. history that laws were passed over a president's wishes. It also showed that Congress could control Reconstruction.

Under the Black Codes, the White League of Louisiana tried to stop black men from voting.

CHAPTER 4

RADICAL REPUBLICANS TAKE CHARGE

In 1866 voters elected many Republicans to Congress. That spring they passed the first Reconstruction Act. The law divided the South into five military districts. Each district had a governor. The law also said the Southern states had to approve the 14th Amendment before their representatives could serve in Congress. Johnson grew frustrated. Radical Republicans had taken over the government.

The Radical Republicans decided that Johnson had to go. They would try to impeach him. If Johnson was no longer president, he could not stop Reconstruction. On February 24, 1868, the House of Representatives voted to impeach Johnson. The case moved to the Senate for trial.

FAST FACTS

Since 1789 more than 10,000 amendments to the Constitution have been proposed. Only 27 of them have been approved by Congress and ratified by the states. The last amendment was added in 1992. It says members of Congress cannot give themselves pay raises before the next election.

impeach: to bring formal charges against a public official who may have committed a crime while in office

FIVE MILITARY DISTRICTS

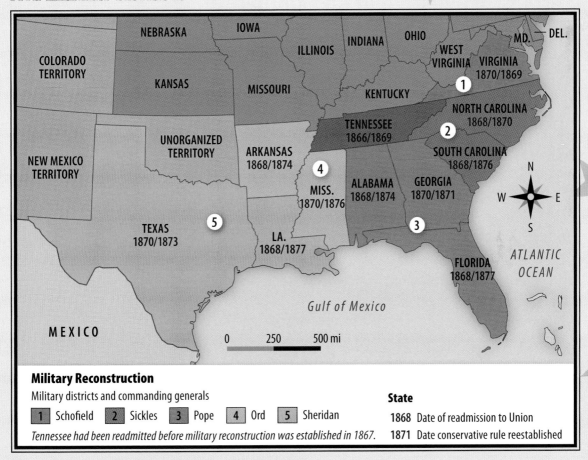

Military Reconstruction

Military districts and commanding generals

| 1 | Schofield | 2 | Sickles | 3 | Pope | 4 | Ord | 5 | Sheridan |

Tennessee had been readmitted before military reconstruction was established in 1867.

State

1868 Date of readmission to Union

1871 Date conservative rule reestablished

The five military districts of the South during Reconstruction

The Radical Republicans thought they had enough votes to impeach Johnson. They needed 36 of 54 senators to vote for Johnson's removal. On May 26 the senators cast their votes. Only 35 votes were cast in favor of impeachment. Johnson stayed in office.

Republicans in the Southern States

The 15th Amendment gave African-Americans voting rights. Each year more and more African-Americans voted. To encourage them to vote, the government sent the army to polling booths. Soldiers were there to keep new voters safe. Most black Americans voted for Republican candidates. In contrast, many whites did not vote at all. More black voters helped Republicans take charge of local and state governments. The Republicans helped repeal the Black Codes. They improved transportation routes and rebuilt homes and buildings. They also expanded public school systems.

Carpetbaggers and Scalawags

Thousands of Americans, white and black, moved from the North to the South during Reconstruction. There were teachers, lawyers, business owners, and army officers. White Southerners called them "carpetbaggers." These Northerners sometimes carried their belongings in small suitcases made of carpet. Some carpetbaggers wanted to make money for themselves. Most truly wanted to help rebuild the South.

Scalawags were Southerners who supported Reconstruction. Many scalawags were poor farmers who had never wanted to leave the Union. They had been against the Civil War. Most Southerners thought scalawags were traitors.

Free black men won the right to vote with the passing of the 15th Amendment.

19

African-Americans in Government

Hundreds of African-Americans won elections at the local and state levels because of Reconstruction. Blacks served alongside whites on juries. They joined school boards. They worked on city councils. Sixteen black men were elected to Congress from 1870 to 1877.

During Reconstruction African-Americans began to serve in government. Hiram R. Revels (right) was the first African-American to serve in Congress.

Reconstruction Ends

By mid-1870 the 11 former Confederate states had returned to the Union. Since the Union was whole again, Congress began to remove federal troops from Southern states. This meant the end of Reconstruction. Americans were not sure about the future. What would happen to the gains made by former slaves? Would the nation keep working for equal rights for all?

FAST FACTS

Mississippi elected the first African-American to serve in Congress. Hiram R. Revels was elected in 1870 and served as senator for one year. In 1871 he became the president of Alcorn University College.

CHAPTER 5

THE SOUTH REBELS

Many Southerners were angry at what the Republicans had done to the South. They resented outsiders trying to change their way of life. They were furious that black Americans had gained rights.

Ku Klux Klan

In 1862 six former Confederate soldiers started a secret club called the Ku Klux Klan. People who joined the Ku Klux Klan were known as Klansmen. They shared many frustrations about Reconstruction. They did not think that former slaves should have the same rights as white people.

Many blacks and their supporters were attacked at night by the Ku Klux Klan.

They wanted to stop black people from going to school. They did not think blacks should have the right to vote. They did not want them to have equal rights at all.

Klansmen were violent. They attacked blacks and their supporters. They dragged victims from their homes. They would beat or even kill them. The Klan sometimes carried torches. They burned down schools and churches attended by African-Americans. These attacks made many black citizens afraid to vote or go to school. In 1870 and 1871 Congress passed laws to control the Klan's violence.

FAST FACTS

The Ku Klux Klan still exists in the United States today. This group still promotes hate against African-Americans and some religious groups, such as Catholics and Jews.

Civil Rights Act of 1875

In 1875 Republicans still had the majority in Congress. They worked hard to pass the Civil Rights Act of 1875. This law gave black Americans the same individual freedoms as whites. It said they could

- ✔ use public transportation
- ✔ eat in restaurants
- ✔ stay in hotels
- ✔ attend theater events

Eight years later the U.S. Supreme Court reviewed the Civil Rights Act of 1875. It said the law focused on individuals, not governments. It struck down the law as unconstitutional. The justices said that Congress could ban discrimination by state governments. However, it could not ban discrimination by individuals.

African-American men were able to serve on juries after the Civil Rights Act of 1875 was passed.

unconstitutional: a law that goes against something set forth in the U.S. Constitution, the document that set up the government of the United States

Shift in Power

Many former Confederate leaders were pardoned during Reconstruction. They went back to their government jobs. Soon the Democrats began to take control of the South. By 1877 Democrats controlled all of the Southern states. At this time the Democratic Party was not for equal rights. This shift in power was a major blow in the fight for equality.

CHAPTER 6

THE END OF RECONSTRUCTION

The presidential election of 1876 forced the Republicans and Democrats to compromise. Twenty electoral votes were questioned. The votes were awarded to the Republican candidate, Rutherford B. Hayes. The Democrats agreed so long as the last troops would leave the South. The Republicans agreed.

The last soldiers left the Southern states in 1877. This marked the end of Reconstruction. It was also the start of a long period of inequality for black Americans.

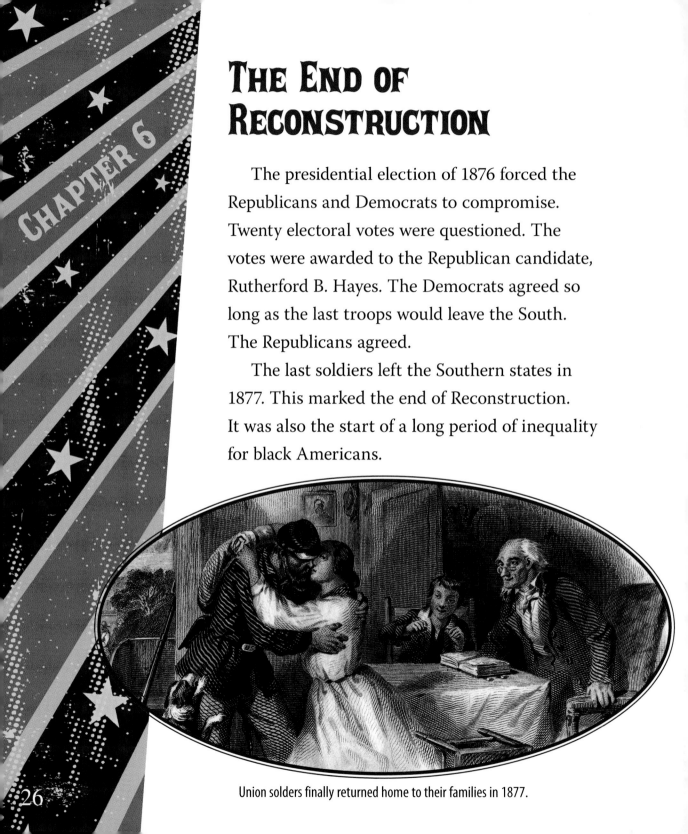

Union solders finally returned home to their families in 1877.

Limiting Freedom

After Reconstruction, Southern states passed laws to keep black and white Americans apart. These laws were called Jim Crow laws. They created segregation across the South. Black Americans could ride public transportation, but they had to sit at the back. They could not go through the front door of a building. They had their own waiting rooms and bathrooms. Black children could not go to school with white children.

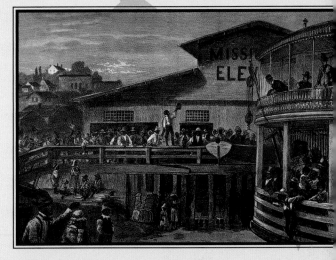

A segregated ship is shown setting sail from Mississippi to New York.

The number of black men who voted dropped. Some states gave reading tests with trick questions. Blacks who failed the tests could not vote. Sometimes they also had to pay a special voting tax. The laws that allowed these inequalities were passed to discriminate against African-Americans.

Black Americans were angry. In response thousands left the South for other states. They still faced prejudice. However, it was not nearly as bad as it was in the South.

segregation: the practice of keeping groups of people apart, especially based on race

prejudice: an opinion about others that is unfair or not based on facts

Legacy of Reconstruction

The Civil War brought freedom, but not equality, for African-Americans. Freed African-Americans often had lives that were little better than slavery. Reconstruction tried to bring about equality but did not succeed.

Life for African-Americans improved little until the civil rights movement of the 1950s and 1960s. Then a new generation of African-American people used the 13th, 14th, and 15th Amendments to demand equal rights. The struggle for equality and understanding between races continues today.

FAST FACTS

In 1995 Mississippi voted to ratify the 13th Amendment, which abolished slavery. However, the state failed to register the result of the vote. The 13th Amendment was finally ratified in February 2013.

Timeline of the Reconstruction Amendments (13, 14, and 15)

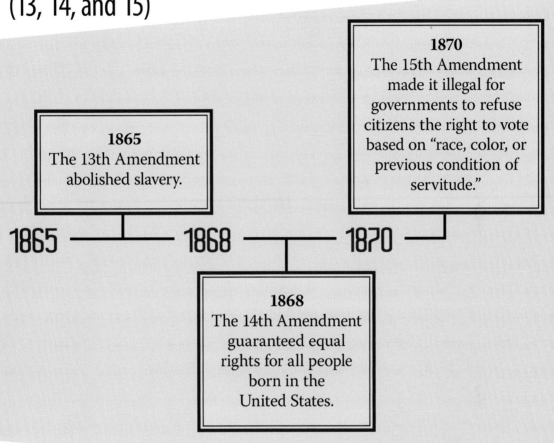

1870
The 15th Amendment made it illegal for governments to refuse citizens the right to vote based on "race, color, or previous condition of servitude."

1865
The 13th Amendment abolished slavery.

1865 —— 1868 —— 1870 ——

1868
The 14th Amendment guaranteed equal rights for all people born in the United States.

29

Glossary

abolish (uh-BOL-ish)—to put an end to something officially

Congress (KAHNG-gruhs)—the government body of the United States that makes laws, made up of the Senate and the House of Representatives

impeach (im-PEECH)—to bring formal charges against a public official who may have committed a crime while in office

oath (OHTH)—a serious, formal promise

pardon (PAHR-duhn)—to forgive someone officially for a serious offense

prejudice (PREJ-uh-diss)—an opinion about others that is unfair or not based on facts

Reconstruction (ree-kuhn-STRUHKT-shuhn)—the period of time, following the Civil War, when the U.S. government tried to rebuild Southern states

secede (si-SEED)—to withdraw formally from a group or an organization, often to form another organization

segregation (seg-ruh-GAY-shuhn)—the practice of keeping groups of people apart, especially based on race

unconstitutional (uhn-kahn-stuh-TOO-shuh-nuhl)—a law that goes against something set forth in the Constitution, the document that set up the government of the United States

veto (VEE-toh)—the power or right to stop a bill from becoming law

Read More

Cooke, Tim. *After the War.* The American Civil War: The Right Answer. New York: Gareth Stevens Pub., 2013.

Fitzgerald, Stephanie. *Reconstruction: Rebuilding America after the Civil War.* The Civil War. Mankato, Minn.: Compass Point Books, 2011.

Howse, Jennifer. *Reconstruction.* Black History. New York: AV2 by Weigl, 2014.

Critical Thinking Using the Common Core

1. Why were the Radical Republicans angry with President Johnson? Give details from the book to explain your answer. What did they do to try to stop him? (Key Ideas and Details)
2. Pick one part of the book that is very important. Why is it important? Use details from the book to explain your answer. (Craft and Structure)
3. On page 28, the author wrote, "Freed African-Americans often had lives that were little better than slavery. Reconstruction tried to bring about equality but did not succeed." What evidence and details are used to support this statement? Do you agree? Explain your thinking. (Integration of Knowledge and Ideas)

Internet Sites

FactHound offers a safe, fun way to find Internet sites related to this book. All of the sites on FactHound have been researched by our staff.

Here's all you do:

Visit *www.facthound.com*

Type in this code: 9781491407240

Super-cool stuff! Check out projects, games, and lots more at www.capstonekids.com

Index

31901056287552